P9-DUC-221

Daffodils at Twilight

Other Books by Margaret Chula

Winter Deepens, Snapshot Press, England (2016)
Just This, Mountains and Rivers Press (2013)
What Remains: Japanese Americans in Internment Camps
    with quilt artist Cathy Erickson, Katsura Press (2009)
The Smell of Rust, Katsura Press (2003)
Always Filling, Always Full, White Pine Press (2001)
Shadow Lines with Rich Youmans, Katsura Press (1999)
Grinding my ink CD
    with Ken Ulansey on woodwinds (1997)
This Moment, Katsura Press (1995)
Grinding my ink, Katsura Press (1993)

Daffodils at Twilight

Poems by

Margaret Chula

Kelsay Books

© 2017 Margaret Chula. All rights reserved. This material may not be reproduced in any form, published, reprinted, recorded, performed, broadcast, rewritten or redistributed without the explicit permission of Margaret Chula. All such actions are strictly prohibited by law.

Cover photograph: David Akoubian
Author photograph: Marq Sutherland
Book design: John A. Hall

ISBN 13: 978-1-945752-51-3

Kelsay Books
Aldrich Press
www.kelsaybooks.com

Acknowledgments

Grateful acknowledgment is made to the following publications in which
    these poems have appeared:

Catamaran Literary Reader: "Song of Gratitude"
Cloudbank: "Elbow of Desire"
Cordella Magazine: "Broken," "Ditching Jesus," and "What I Wanted"
Kyoto Journal: "Artichoke" and "I Love the Way"
Modern Haiku: "Talking Tina" and "Polishing the Spoons"
Naugatuck River Review: "Nana's Pantry"
Spillway: "Feral"
Sufi Journal: "Vespers"
Tiger's Eye: "I Love the Way"
U.S. 1 Worksheets: "Hoping Daddy Will Bring Home the Milk"
VoiceCatcher: "Still Life With Cabbage" and "A Night on Broomsticks"
    (previously titled "Fishtail")

The following poems have been included in anthologies or received awards:

"Talking Tina," "Still Life With Cabbage," and "Polishing
    the Spoons" received Pushcart Prize nominations, 2013
"Feral," received a Pushcart Prize nomination, 2016
"In the Garden," in *The Poeming Pigeon: Poems from the Garden,*
    The Poetry Box, 2017
"The Good Sister" in *The Knotted Bond: Poems About Sisters,*
    edited by Liz Nakazawa, Uttered Chaos Press, 2013
"Still Life With Cabbage" in *She Holds the Face of the World:
    Ten Years of VoiceCatcher, 2015*
"Cutouts" in the *Oregon State Poetry Association Anthology,* 2014
 "A Light Fandango," First Prize in the Jackson's Books
    Poetry Contest, 2004
"Polishing the Spoons," Second Prize in the Dancing Poetry
    Contest, 2011
"Ritual" received an Honorable Mention in the Haiku Society
    of America's International Haibun Contest, 2015
"Inheritance" was a Runner-Up in The 2nd Biennial Phyllis
    Ennes Poetry Contest and printed as a broadside
    for the 2016 Skagit River Poetry Festival.

Many thanks to my mentors and dear friends in Word Sisters and the Pearl Poets: Christine Delea, Cindy Williams Guttierrez, Diane Holland, Andrea Hollander, Paulann Petersen, Donna Prinzmetal, Joanna Rose, Penelope Scambly Schott, and Suzanne Sigafoos. My heartfelt gratitude and love to Andrea Hollander for suggestions on selecting and ordering the poems. For the gift of time and a tranquil setting to work in, I am indebted to the Helene Wurlitzer Foundation, the Vermont Studio Center, Hypatia-in-the-Woods, and Playa for writing residencies and fellowships. And, lastly, where would I be without John, my partner in life and creativity, my stalwart supporter, and technical angel.

Contents

II. Daffodils at Twilight

III. Inheritance

For my mother Adelia

and siblings

Kathleen, David, Stephen, and Deborah

I. Marking Time

Artichoke

When you handed me an artichoke,
you held it like a small porcupine
in the palm of your hand, its roped stem
anchored to your heart line.

This was your first offering: an exotic
vegetable from the fields of Pescadero,
harvested by farmworkers
with sunburnt hands.

Your hands were tender, peeling back each leaf
its soft flesh coming off willingly, as later
my patchouli-scented clothes would be removed
and my own flesh savored.

I haven't mentioned the artichoke's heart
enclosed in its bristly wrapper, the damp thistle
needing to be removed before the succulence
before the most enticing pleasure.

I haven't mentioned your heart or the way artichokes
smell of sex and, forty years later, how your skin
smells like dry sawdust.

I haven't told you that every time I eat an artichoke,
I look at the teeth marks left in the discarded leaves
and am still hungry.

Still Life With Cabbage

In the yellow kitchen, the cabbage is boiling. The pot is black where flames have bruised it. A woman is wearing a bib apron, her hair pulled back with bobby pins. The rubber ends are missing. They scrape her scalp when she sticks them in. Once she used to pin curl her hair before going dancing at the Bernardston Inn. Once she used to sing *It Had To Be You*. And then it *was* him, and then, five children wailing and burping and spitting up on her apron—the canvas one with the tie-on straps that harness her to the kitchen. Now she reaches for the ladle, thinking about the sheets, wet and clumped in the washing machine. And then later, when her husband comes home, his silhouette dark and sullen beneath the covers—whiskey breath that will make her gag and turn away. Now she's turning the hamburgers. The sizzle and spit sting her wrists. She wipes the grease on her apron, adding to the stains of beets, pureed peas, and the swollen buds of Brussels sprouts that no one would ever touch.

Hoping Daddy Will Bring Home the Milk

You're darn tootin' we loved Fig Newtons
   Devil Dogs, angel hair, and most of all
      Chef Boy-Ar-Dee ravioli.

We loved collecting Popsicle sticks on Conway Street
   and washing them in our swimming pool
      with blue fishes painted on the side

the pool where our cat Lulu drowned
   her grave strewn with Queen Anne's lace
      those pinwheels a tilt-a-whirl to Heaven.

Kathy and I were junk-skunks
weaving Popsicle sticks into lattices
   and coloring them with Crayola crayons:
      carnation pink, goldenrod, and sky blue

then hawking them on the sidewalk
along with hydrangea burgers
   from Hazel Tombs' yard
     to get us some
       trash-cash.

We were the tow-headed twosome
upbeat sisters tootin' our horns
   so we wouldn't hear
     the dull rumble
      of hunger
       in our bellies.

Home Sweet Home

She is pinning a feather to her cloche hat,
the puce-colored one that reminds her
of the diapers of her fifth baby, now colicky,
now sleeping, after stuttering like a machine gun
through every room of the house.

Stan is out again. He's lifting a Budweiser to his lips,
laughing with his teammates about his fastball pitch
that aced the game.

She is gliding a peacock plume across her face,
fanning the rage that boils like this morning's
coffee that percolated out of control—beyond
the kitchen walls and under the porch steps
where it hid in the dark.

He will return in the middle of the night
hammering his fist against the locked door
heaving his bloated body that will never
fit through the keyhole.

She is caressing her breasts with the feather,
muffling her cries in the throw pillow—
the one embroidered with *Home Sweet Home.*

Now she is dipping the shaft of the feather
into the spilt coffee grounds,
grouting them into the cracks
of her lifeline.

One Afternoon When I'm Eight

I sneak off
into the woods
with four older boys.

Beneath a bridge,
they form a huddle
around me—beg me
to take off
my underpants.

I slip off
the wrappers
of my Juicy Fruit gum
and show them
how to weave
a gum wrapper chain.

We wander in the woods
till it's nearly dark.
None of us
will admit
that we're lost.

When I finally get home
I'm ready
to confess my sins.

In the dining room
my younger brothers
are fitting Tinker Toy pegs
into their spools.

In our bedroom,
my sister kneels
on the chenille rug
arranging outfits
for her paper dolls.

Mother's in the kitchen
slicing green beans
for supper.

She sends me to Daddy.
He's usually not here,
but today he's sprawled
on the couch
drinking a beer.

Through the din
of a Red Sox game
I tell him about getting lost
with the boys.

He pats me on the head
and hands me
a quarter.

Baby Deborah
wails from the playpen.

Nobody noticed
I'd been gone—
not even my cat
perched
on the window sill

staring down
the darkness.

Dobra

Neighbors stared out their windows
that late February day when we left
the yellow house on Conway Street,
the snow hard and dirty.

Papa's pickup idled in the driveway.
Mother loaded cardboard boxes into the back.
My four brothers and sisters were in cars too—
Aunt Betty's, Aunt Jean's, and Uncle Joe's.

It was a family affair, leaving Daddy
that beer-drinking, card-playing ne'er-do-well.
I sat next to Papa with his happy whiskers.
Dobra, dobra, he said to me. Good, good.

I held Fluffy tight in my lap.
Her purring warmed my belly.
I thought about Daddy and how
I would miss our Friday nights

eating pickled pigs' feet and listening
to *The Shadow* on the radio. I imagined him
coming home with his empty lunch box
and finding my note on the kitchen table:

Gone to live at Nana and Papa's.
Hope to see you soon.

Arithmetic

Fourth grade is hard and even harder when your mother leaves
your father forever. The next day you're in a new school sitting
at an old wooden desk with an inkwell filled with real ink and knife
scratches everywhere from kids who live in Northfield Farms
and milk cows before coming to school.

On that first day in the new school, you wear an ironed white blouse,
plaid skirt, and black buckle-up boots. Miss Forbes is teaching long
division and, even though you memorized your multiplication tables
at the other school, long division is hard. Especially figuring out
what to do with remainders.

As you're trying to divide 365 by 6, a boy named Harry moves
his chair closer. You can smell his Ivory soap skin and you want
him to say something—anything. You want a sign that he'll be
your friend and, just as you're thinking this, a big drop of ink
splatters on your sleeve. You watch it bleed into the fabric.
You look at Harry's red face as he says *I'm sorry* and think:
now we can be friends.

Your other friend is the Dickinson Memorial Library.
You can't wait to open those heavy doors, greet Mrs. Phelps
at the front desk, and head straight for the window seat,
plush with pillows. Your reading cave. Across the room,
the grandfather clock's reliable tick and gong on the half hour
remind you that it will soon be dark and you'll have to ride
your bike home to help Mother set the table. Only six places now.
Today you understand why subtraction is easier than division.

That First Summer at the Farm

I wake up to robin song and the smell of doughnuts
sizzling in Nana's skillet and when I go outside,

the horses in Mr. Mroczyk's pasture whinny
and shake their manes loose of flies,

those sticky manes that I want to braid
like my own hair tied with green ribbons

so it doesn't get tangled when I ride my two-wheeler
down the sidewalk pretending I'm Annie Oakley

chasing outlaws, the Jack of Spades playing card
click-clacking in the spokes as I pedal faster and faster

to Mary Anna's house where she shows me a black widow
in her web and we wait for the spider to mate with the male

and then bite off his head as we heard they do, but
after an hour we're bored and check out the sidewalk

where there's a banana slug oozing slime that we dip
our fingers into, then press together, glued tight

like the two dogs we saw stuck to each other
until Kay Luciw threw water on them and then

at us for laughing, which we did a lot of that summer—
spitting out watermelon seeds, smoking green pipes

from Nana's pipe vine, and walking barefoot in the grass,
always, *always* looking for four-leaf clovers

that, if I was lucky enough,
would bring Mother and Daddy back together.

A Light Fandango

On hot summer afternoons, Nana spread out sheets
on the parlor floor for Kathy and me to take our naps.

The sheets smelled of sunshine, the furniture of must.
Our lips tasted of strawberries.

We stripped down to our panties, the shades drawn—
no neighbors anyway—our chests rosy and flat
shoulders marked by swimsuit lines.

Kathy squirmed. Hot skin grazing mine, I snapped
and then we settled down singing our repertoire
of Roger Williams' tunes from Mother's LP.

When we woke up, Nana put in a piano roll
shot full of holes, like moth bites
in our winter coats, but these held music.

The piano sweetened and the ivories rippled with joy.
Up and down the keyboard, black keys like men in tuxedos
danced a light fandango with ladies in white gowns.

We pumped till our legs ached and the piano roll zipped
up tight as a window shade, the afternoon sun pulsing
through the cracks, coloring our arms with zebra stripes.

Talking Tina

I hated the doll Mother gave me for Christmas 1957, the year she left Daddy and got her old job back working at the Mount Hermon Post Office. That Christmas she said we could each have one expensive present. I asked for a Talking Tina doll, whose arms and legs had joints that clicked into new positions. She could kneel, kick, throw, and wave. And when you pulled a string at the back of her neck, she would say: *Hi, I'm Tina* or *Do you want to dance?* Tina had pointy breasts and long legs. I'd seen her at Woolworth's, smiling behind the cellophane in her box. My younger sister wanted a doll, too, but hadn't decided which one. On Christmas day, we both ran for the big boxes and tore off the wrapping paper. I got a doll all right, but she had brown hair—not blonde—and her arms and legs had no joints. Kathy had Talking Tina! I yanked my doll out of her box and began twisting her rubbery arms and legs into grotesque shapes. Mother was watching me from across the room. I held it up and shouted *Look what an ugly doll you gave me!* Kathy smiled and pulled the string. Talking Tina said: *Do you want to dance?*

Papa's Polka

Papa came from Bialystok, a place he never
spoke of once he settled in the New World
where he worked eighty acres of tobacco,
squash, corn—crops of the natives.

At day's end, he trudged in from the fields
to take a bath with water that Nana had heated
on the wood-burning stove—then slumped
into his favorite chair by the kitchen window.

Sputnik! Shitty, shitty two by four!

I laughed at his outbursts, then jumped on his lap
to play with the buckles on his bib overalls. Every night,
he'd crack an egg yolk into his beer mug and suck it down.
Foam sudsed his whiskers. Soon he would spin the dials
on the radio until static rippled into polkas.

And we'd dance—Papa lifting and twirling me dizzy
while Nana clicked her knitting needles faster and faster.
Forgotten was the day when his workhorses reared up,
startled by the beep—beep—beep of a Mercedes Benz
driven by the town doctor's reckless daughter.

Forgotten was the crack of his skull on the pavement
the years of confusion that followed—
    amnesia, blackouts, and then those outbursts
       in between
when the radio was silent
and we were alone in the dark kitchen
and he would shout at the top of his lungs

Shitty, shitty two by four. Khrushchev through the outhouse door!

Trout Fishing with My Brothers

Even though I'm the oldest, I'm the girl
so I dilute strawberry Zyrex with water,
pour it into Army surplus canteens,
and make peanut butter and jelly sandwiches
careful not to tear the Wonder Bread.

My brothers carry the fish basket, their poles,
and the can of worms.
We make our way
through Papa's cornfields
to Davis's brook
and space ourselves
along the bank.

I sit down in the dirt, bait my hook,
and wipe the worm guts off
on my shorts.
Casting the line
as they taught me,
I wait for a bite.

Bored, I start singing
How much is that doggie in the window (arf, arf)?
"Shut up," David shouts,
"you're scaring away the fish."
Then a yank on the line.
I've hooked a huge one.
"Sucker," Stephen says.
"Throw it back. Trout's
what we're after."

I reel in sucker
after sucker.

Prying the hook
out of its fleshy jaw,
I begin to feel sorry
for this unpopular fish.

Unwanted,
like a flabby aunt
who shows up
uninvited
and talks your ear off.

My brothers catch seven trout.
They line up their trophies
fin to fin in the woven basket,
a fraternity of fish.
Their rainbow backs glisten.

Fairy Dust

On Halloween, I'm Tinker Bell, dazzling in green chiffon
and crinoline slips—hand-me-down gowns from the Blasbergs,
the rich Jewish family down the street.

Crowned with a tiara from the Five & Dime and sporting
silver slippers on my feet, I clutch a magic wand and a bag
of Ivory Flakes. Fairy dust.

I want to make everyone happy: Mrs. Tombs who's fat and
crabby, Mr. Jacobs who broke his leg falling off the roof,
and the blind lady down the street who, with just a sprinkle
of my fairy dust, will be able to watch *The Price is Right*.

I carry magic in my bag. No black cat can jinx me—no cracks
stepped on in the dark. I know there are witches in the world.
Evil women who tell lies about Mother. Women who hate
children because they have too many or none at all.

But I also know that I can reach into my bag and sprinkle
fairy dust over them, my arms arcing in the night
dusting them like a blessing, feathers
of Ivory Flakes washing them clean.

Adelia

It is what it is.

Morning sickness
I hold on tight to the kitchen sink
to the smooth, cold porcelain.
    After the shoving match
        the crushed smell of petunias.

Tulip bulbs I planted in spring
their leaves flapping inside out.
    The five seeds he ejaculates
    in winter–winter–spring–spring–winter
    all sprout to life
    stunning me
    with their small needs.

Blizzard of cotton diapers
how they freeze on the clothesline,
turn to rags by spring.

Those poor goldfish we carried home
in plastic bags, disappear
down the toilet
before they can be named.
    That putrid smell in the glass bowl
    with food flakes floating on top.

My little ones
in sun suits with seashell patterns
and suntan lines on their shoulders
make castles in the sandbox—
    the closest they'll ever come
    to the seashore.

Youngest child at home with measles.
    We snuggle under blankets
    on the couch where she was conceived
    and watch afternoon soaps.
    As the World Turns.

My son brings me a handful of dandelions
with serrated leaves
like blades of a buzz saw
ripping through deadwood.
    My husband now resigned as sawdust.
    Dandelion fluff glides through the afternoon.

On my Olivetti, I list all the reasons
for leaving him. Consonants splatter
like insects across the onionskin.
    My eldest daughter stands behind me
    tweezing out new gray hairs.

Varicose veins stipple my legs.
    A newly divorced woman
    serving home-style dinners
    at Vielmetti's Italian Restaurant
    to my friends
        who pull up
        in shiny black Buicks.

Another chance.
I wash my feet in the farmhouse sink,
the one with the rusty drain.
    Will he caress me tonight,
    a divorcee with five kids?

That nightmare again—
lost in the funhouse.
    Clack of cart wheels
    stench
    of cardboard pop-ups
    taste of sulfur
    the inescapable heat.

I want my mother
to come back from the dead
and tell me
    It's going to be all right.

Nana's Pantry

I was safe in Nana's pantry, behind the door
screened with her crocheted curtains.
It was my hiding place, dark cave
of Fig Newtons and spicy cinnamon
spilt like pollen on the flour barrel.

Here was the vinegar for coloring Easter eggs,
cloves we poked into apples for pomanders,
molasses that turned the gingerbread men brown,
vanilla extract to dab behind my ears. Cucumbers
floated in Mason jars, content as sea slugs.

I sniffed every jar—sauerkraut, marmalade, peppermint,
the vocabulary of my grandmother who spoke no English.
Sitting on the green and beige squares of the linoleum floor,
I ate the round bellybuttons of Nana's doughnuts,
broke the backs of walnuts with a silver nutcracker.

Now my mother tells me *her* story about hiding in the pantry.
How she waited till nobody was around, and then used a fork
to pry a black velvet ribbon off the end of a whiskbroom.
How the fork slipped and stabbed her in the eye.
How she was too scared to scream or ask for help.

I would have helped her, the two of us huddled on the floor.
I would have mixed together a balm for her eye, a poultice
to calm her fear. And then, I'd tear off a piece of bread
from Nana's still-warm loaf, spread it with jam and honey
and butter—so sweet and soft and forgiving.

Quarantine

I turn thirteen and come down with scarlet fever.
My face and neck are flushed, my throat sore, tongue swollen.
Every day, the red bead on the thermometer rises.

I'm a prisoner inside this bed of blankets. The iron bed frame
creaks every time I thrash. Mother's brow is always furrowed,
her mouth hidden by a white mask, hands protected by gloves.
She serves me tomato soup and Saltines that I cannot swallow.
For twelve days, I wear nothing but gray flannel pajamas.

For comfort, I turn to the jar of honey. Like an addict, I spoon
the thick syrup down my throat. When I can speak, I make up
stories about the fabrics in the squares of Nana's patchwork
quilt. Outside my bedroom door, my brothers play with
their Lionel train set.

Staring at cracks in the ceiling of the New England farmhouse,
I see profiles looking back. People I don't know follow me
into dreams. Even before I finish reading *Little Women,*
I know that *I* will be the one to die of scarlet fever.

I read Nancy Drew mysteries, too, but now they depress me,
bound to this bed with the smell of dust from Nana's curtains.
As soon as I finish reading a book, Mother takes it down
to the cellar and burns it in the furnace.

Cutouts

The only horses I liked were cookie cutouts.
I loved the way that dough stuck to the sharp
metallic edges, even after you lifted the mold.

Nana flattened out the dough with her wooden
rolling pin and sprinkled it with flour so the small
horses had a mottled look—like appaloosas

who had pranced in a snowfield after dark
free of the weight of men and saddles
and bad-tempered children.

I don't know why Nana had horse cookie cutters.
She never liked real horses with their neighing
and unpredictable ways.

My first pony ride was at summer camp.
His nostrils snorted. Flies buzzed around his tail.
He stank of dust and dung.

I bounced high off the saddle. My bony legs turned
numb from gripping. The reins tore my skin. I cried
with relief when I was allowed to dismount.

The next time Nana made horse cookies
I bit off all four of their legs, one by one
with my small, sharp teeth.

What I Wanted

All my life, I wanted to ride bareback on a tiger through
the jungles of Borneo, to race by warthogs gorging on
pineapples, past headhunters with their poisonous darts
sheathed, mouths agape.

I wanted to outstrip Lady Godiva—her everlasting tresses,
her smirk of satisfaction shocking even Adam and Eve
as they cavorted in their own pleasure.

I wanted to be a swan on a lake in Shangri-La, folding
my wings around a lover as I glided past frogs, their lips
puckered like princes' before they plopped into mud.

I longed to find paradise in a place. To lie in a hammock
on the island of Boracay, swaddled in a sarong, reading
Lady Chatterley's Lover while peeling back the bruised
skins of mangosteens.

Instead, I spent my childhood looking out at an ash pile
in the back yard where Nana would empty ashes
from the wood stove and later toss in the limp kitten
run over by a speeding car on Bennett Meadow Road.

I made my heaven on King Philip's Hill—building a fort,
shooting arrows into the spines of birches, galloping
on my imaginary pony down the Mayflower Trail.

Instead, I passed my thirteenth summer on Maple Street
lying in the grass reading about Scarlett and Rhett
and her beloved plantation, my tomboy knees hidden
beneath pedal pushers waiting for the moment

when I'd peel off the scabs and begin to live.

Marking Time

On King Philip's Hill, someone may find
the remains of our messages tucked into
the stumps of two-hundred-year-old trees.

Four children, wild in the woods—the ferment
of moldering leaves, the sweet giddiness
of mayflowers spanning our days.

We heard the Wampanoags breathing
beneath their burial mounds. Tomahawks
and arrowheads punctuated their war cries

as they paddled up the Connecticut River,
then trod through a wilderness of oak burrs,
acorns, wintergreen, and hoarfrost.

They are gone now. We are grown, the hill
overrun with ivy strangling the birch trees
whose bark we peeled to scribble urgent notes

Snake on Maple Trail
Indians attacking at dawn
Meet at fort

Birch bark preserved our memories
in parchment—afternoons when we put
ear to hollow trunk, mouths opened

to rain, small hands prying back
the hoods of jack-in-the-pulpits
to witness the miracle.

Small Town Girl

Northfield, Massachusetts

The town I grew up in has a soda fountain
where old men in suspenders sit on red vinyl stools
sipping root beer floats through paper straws.

The grocery store smells of kielbasa and Pine-Sol.
Shirley, the cashier, styles her hair in a bouffant
with spit curls like parentheses around her face.

There's a Creamie, too, with butterscotch dips.
My sister and I change into pedal pushers and race
our bikes up Main Street hoping to meet boys.

Mornings, we wait for the bus at Morgan's Garage.
The rainbow smell of gasoline fills the silence
between me and Buddy, the boy next door.

My sister and I save up babysitting money to buy
candy-striped wallpaper for our bedroom. Sanitary pads
wait in their pink box like presents to be unwrapped.

In my underwear drawer, I hide newspaper clippings
of Li'l Abner comics—my secret obsession
with Daisy Mae's cleavage.

And under the mattress, my diary written in shorthand
so my sister can't read about how I spy on Buddy
mowing the lawn, the tug of his hips in skin-tight jeans.

Blame It on Daisy Mae

the way her breasts ballooned like half globes
from the rim of her polka-dotted blouse

the way she romped barefoot, long legs
beneath a cropped skirt, golden mane
tossing like a filly's.

My hair was blonde, my twelve-year-old
breasts like half-risen bread dough
with tiny pink buttons.

I'd discovered the pleasure button years before
while sitting on the washing machine
during the rinse cycle, and later

on afternoons spent with L'il Abner
comic strips of Daisy Mae's cleavage, my legs
straddling a pillow—riding it—cheeks aglow

as my breath came fast and short
like Black Beauty's just before
he cleared the hurdles.

Sometimes, I'd climb on top of my sister
as she lay face down on her bed
reading a romance—her fanny

a saddle I rode, this compliant steed
that never bucked or whinnied
as I plied her with chitchat.

Afterwards, I'd roll off
and smooth out the puckers
from the blue chenille bedspread
that left dimples on her face.

Phys Ed

Phys Ed. Sex Ed. Driver's Ed.
Who was this guy Ed who made us do all these things
in high school? *Mandatory. For your own good and safety.*

Those red gym outfits with metal-toothed belts,
nubbled cotton socks, sneakers—always white.
We looked like cheerleaders, but were not at all cheerful
as we dribbled the basketball back and forth
across the court, racing each other
bam, bam, bam

or climbed the ropes—*touch the ceiling and shinny down*
our legs pretzel-wrapped around the rough jute, like
when we had to hold our pee, then pushing up, up, up
the strain on our arms and legs.
Preparation for sex.

And the most boring sport: running track.
The two-mile course was a circuit
through pastures and woodlands.
Susan and I knew the short cuts back to school
and how to squirt water on our faces
and on the backs of our gym clothes
to look like sweat.

Then on to the locker room to peel off
our soaked clothes, the combination lock
that I never quite believed would open,
the rubber Playtex girdle stinking up my locker,
those threadbare towels from home,
and lime green soap Mother bought
in an economy bag at the A&P.

The towel barely covered my thin body.
No breasts, no pubic hair, no
confidence as I slunk
to the shower stall in the far corner.

The shower room smelled
of everyone else's
gold-label Dial soap.

Ed, the taskmaster, did not teach us
how to deal with envy.

He now lives in a tiny locker
in a chamber of my heart.
Sometimes he bangs on the door,
but mostly he's quiet.

When I figure out the combination,
I'll let him out.

II. Daffodils at Twilight

Fifty Years Later, Mother and Daughter Stop by
307 Conway Street

"Geez, somebody needs to mow the lawn. Remember when you ran
across the yard to your father and you fell on a stick and cut your tongue?
Maybe you were too young to remember that. Anyway, he went crazy—
picked you up and rushed you to the hospital.
You really loved your father."

> *I remember the huge walnut tree in the front yard.*
> *When I was nine, I gathered nuts and stored them*
> *in the pantry to feed my brothers and sisters in case*
> *we ran out of food. Now I'm sixty, my siblings*
> *have scattered, and there's no sign of the tree.*

"The front porch is still there. I loved that porch, especially in summer
when I'd sit on the glider and rock my babies to sleep. And those glass
bottles of milk delivered to the front door each morning. Fresh milk,
with cream on top for my coffee. Your father was so jealous. He thought
I was having an affair with the milkman. Can you imagine that?"

> *I stare at the window seat where I sat with my baby*
> *brother playing "London Bridge is Falling Down"*
> *on the Victrola. I felt safe there with sunlight streaming*
> *through the crocheted curtains that smelled of bleach*
> *and reminded me of Nana and Papa's farmhouse*
> *where Mother took us after she left Daddy.*

"There's the clothesline your father made so I could hang out diapers.
For years, I'd have to run them through the wringer washing machine
and hang them on the line with those wood clothespins. Can you imagine
doing that now? The clothes would freeze stiff in the winter. With every
new baby, Stan had to add another line. One-two-three-four-five. God!
How did I ever do it?

I remember when we got the automatic washing machine.
On Monday washdays, I'd climb up and sit on top of it
during the rinse cycle. All that jiggling made me feel
tingly, like when I sneaked upstairs to Mother
and Daddy's bedroom and wriggled facedown
on her embroidered throw pillow
until the waterfalls came.

"Your father never spent any money on what he called 'luxuries.'
Like food on the table for you kids. We only went shopping once
a week—on Friday, when he got his paycheck. When we ran out
of food, that was it. I don't know what I would've done without
your Aunt Jean who brought vegetables from her garden."

Hazel Tombs' hydrangea bushes with their heavy lavender blooms
that Kathy and I lopped off, then pressed between two leaves
and tried to sell as hamburgers at a sidewalk stand
to make some extra money for Mother.

"I have to admit, the house looks pretty good now. Someone's
repainted it after all these years. Just like when your father
gussied it up, trying to get us to move back. A lot of good
that did. Thank God, I got you kids away from him.
You're much better off without a father.

The swing that Daddy put up for me in the backyard.
The sound of hammer on wood, smell of jute
the feel of wind on my face as I soared away
from the house on Conway Street.

A Night on Broomsticks

In my favorite dream, I'm flying
with Mother on broomsticks

our hair swirling and knotting
in the wind and—

what the hell, we don't care
we're above it all—

dropping white powder on our enemies
dusting the crops of dullards

& drunkards & men
who have poisoned our hearts.

We are the sirens of morning
the restless windmills at noon

devious daughters skulking at dusk
our laughter so loud

that even the ravens retreat
to the crotches of pines.

Here we are again—Mother and I
  flying faster and faster

    fluttering our fishtail feet
      pummeling

        those outstretched hands
          that try to drag us down.

Inventory

At age 92, Mother moves out of the Church Street Home for Women

three bags of rags washed to death, the pink roses and bluebirds
barely visible

plastic bags from every store she shopped in over the past
thirteen years

a bag of bags, each one with a string handle, all decorated
with cheerful motifs

manila envelopes with their flaps glued shut, all tied up neatly
with white string

60 blouses, some with yellow age stains

1 dickey from another century

10 coats and jackets, several with money in the pockets

10 pocketbooks with no money in them

50 pairs of slacks, waistlines saggy with stretched elastic

hundreds of hangers that she sorts, ties up, and agrees to give away

a set of golf clubs that she can no longer carry

2 leggy, half-dead wandering jews in pots too high to water

a wooden clothes drying rack with the white paint peeling off

every letter and postcard I sent her for the past forty-five years

all the memories in this room that she must leave behind

The Arbors Assisted Living Entrance Exam

Good afternoon and welcome to The Arbors. Would you please tell me your full name.
Adelia Dorothy Chula. But don't tell anyone my middle name.
I hate the name Dorothy.

Okay. Can you tell me the name of the current president?
Barack Obaaaama!

Very good. And the last president?
I won't say what I thought of him, but his name was Bussssshhh.

That's right. Now for some food questions. Do you have any food allergies?
No. But I like a low-salt, low-fat diet. Can you do that for me?
And I hate liver! I'll leave the table if there's liver there.

Can you chew your food or would you like it mashed up for you?
I can chew fine. Do you have bread and butter plates?

Yes, of course. Do you need help cutting your meat?
No, I can cut fine. Just make sure the knives are sharp.

Okay, now, breakfast. What do you usually eat for breakfast, Adelia?
Orange juice, toast, and coffee. But I'll eat eggs sometimes
if they're not fried. Do you have tablecloths on the table
for all your meals?

*Yes, we do. Now some information about your room. We'll strip your bed
every week and make it up with new linens.*
Pillowcases too?

*Yes, of course. We usually come by every night and tap on your door to
make sure you're okay before you go to sleep. Does that work for you?*
No, never mind. I don't want anybody bothering me at night.
Sometimes I have curlers in my hair.

Now, Adelia, do you have any questions for us?
Yeah. Did I pass the exam?

Yes, you passed with flying colors. And I know you'll be a fine addition to The Arbors.
Good, because I've gotta get home. Judge Judy's on at 4:00.

Since You Asked

Yes, her cheekbones are still high
and her complexion clear, but pale

her hands riddled with wrinkles.
But her fingernails are still long

in case that interests you—no more
scrubbing laundry on a washboard

for her five kids. And since you asked
about her mood, I would say it's troubling

like a squall that comes up suddenly
on a summer's day and drenches

the laundry hanging on a clothesline
that her ex-husband made. And him

well he's just a bag of bones laid out
in a coffin in his dry-cleaned suit.

Let me tell you more about Mother,
her small pleasures at the end of life:

the squirrel that skitters up the tree
outside the nursing home window,

the slippers her daughter coaxes onto
her swollen feet, necklaces that perfectly

match her blouses, her favorite lipstick
only half gone. And, since you asked

if she believes in the afterlife, I can tell you
that her idea of heaven is being buried

in St. Mary's Cemetery surrounded
by gravestones for her five children.

If you stop by her room to visit,
she'd like that. Be sure to admire

the gourd on her nightstand—
its warped and enduring beauty.

In Her Ninety-Fifth Year

she is still like a swallowtail
yellow wings neatly folded
into hospital gray
her free flights
monitored
by buzzers
summoning
weary women
in white uniforms
into the small room
where she sips nectar
from a long plastic tube.

Mother has ended her flight,
her swirls and swoops
in the sunlit garden.
No honey touches her lips.
Antennae collapsed into silence,
she feels the net closing in, closing in.

Autumn with Birds

Morning rain is tender, inviting me to slow down. How it taps
the leaves before their final fall. Distant mountains obscured
by fog are still there, even though I can't see them.

Will Mother die in autumn, hands nested in her lap, knuckles
veined and buckled like the leaves of sugar maples?
The bird feeder outside her window is empty.

Once she told me she dreamt of dancing in her wedding dress
to a Glenn Miller tune. She woke up to cricket song.
I have given away all her slippers.

Tonight, while picking white hairs from my brush, I think of
Yu Xuang's mother who was troubled because her daughter
talked to flowers. Not *my* mother.

Together we mimicked bird songs, ridiculously happy when
they called back—robins, chickadees, and even a bittern
hidden in cattails. From the front porch, we mocked
its deep-throated gurgle.

Childhood summers, a screech owl slipped its lullaby
through my open window. I leaned out in my nightgown
to reply, but the owl was too far away to hear.

I learned the mourning dove's song when I lived in Japan.
Its cooing on rainy afternoons sounded like damp futons,
clammy and musty. Always in pairs, what could they
be mourning?

I know what I will mourn. The lost birds, their songs forgotten.
My mother's voice that I could never imitate. The blue glass
bird she gave me on my window sill, earthbound and mute.

Gone

Adelia Chula 1915-2012

no more dentures and infected gums
no more pills and injections
no more night diapers and stale urine
no more bruises or broken legs
no more walker or wheelchair
no more physical therapy where you try 110%
no more searching for words that have disappeared
no more mistaking your son for your dead brother
no more hallucinations of spiders crawling on your arms
no more pureed food that you can't identify
no more pulleys to get you on and off the toilet

gone your brothers and sisters, your friends too
gone the waking and screaming in terror
the weeping without knowing why
gone the desire to talk or eat
or change into the pink blouse the nurse holds up
gone any hope that things will get better

Where You Go When You Want to Hide

I.
Crawl into the tiny closet with your dead mother's clothes.
Press your nose into fabric, into all that's left of skin, now
turned to dust clumped like nightmares beneath your bed.

Climb inside the cedar chest, beckoning you like a coffin.
Close the lid and curl up, round as an avocado seed
or the tender lychee safe inside its puckered rind.

II.
Creep like a luna moth into the pulp of manzanita.
Compress your crepe de chine wings until they
become your second skin, useless for flight.

Sink into luscious mud, warm and soft as your mother's
embrace. Hold your breath until the ache begins for real
until it begs for release, like the whip-poor-will
flying into the wild blue yonder.

Daffodils at Twilight

This is the pulse that makes your blood surge,
makes you remember bouquets for your mother

held in small fists of wanting to please,
of waiting to hear her say again

You are the kindest of all my children.
You are my number one daughter.

And the gray of winter vanishes—
disappears like your grief

into ritual and reams of poems.

Now you know better than to cut
those blossoms, their scent

a reminder of moon phases
and seasons

and how their petals will turn
to parchment

like the withered arms
of your mother.

As the crickets sing their night song,
you stand by the window

needing to hear those words
You are my number one daughter.

Still,
this terrible hunger.

Ritual

is a meditation bowl, candle, incense, and a statue of Buddha
that I bought at a temple market in Kyoto. Every week,
I place a seasonal flower in the miniature vase. Today
it's a camellia, red as blood, as fire, as energy
that has drained from me into its petals.

I rearrange everything on the altar to make room
for the lacquerware box holding a Ziploc bag labeled
"Remains of Adelia Chula." When I first held them,
weeks after she died, they still felt warm. I want them
to smell like the cedar ashes of my incense or like
Mother's baby-powder skin. But they're just
crushed bones, acrid remains scraped
from the belly of the incinerator.

In Japan, after the beloved has been cremated,
family members use long-stemmed chopsticks
to pick out a few bones. They are searching for
the throat bone, a tiny bone inside the Adam's
apple that looks like a Buddha, to bring home
and place on the family altar

        collecting dust
        on the window sill
        last year's wishbone

First Anniversary

A year after your death, while stirring soup
at the kitchen stove, I listen to a program

on the radio about how to let the dying go—
and I remember how deserted I felt

when you began curling into yourself,
wanting that darkness more than me.

Today I took the ornaments off the noble fir,
now frail with brittle limbs, and I thought

about the day we buried you in St. Mary's Cemetery,
how your great-granddaughter took your necklaces

out of her treasure box and draped them,
one by one, around each of our necks.

How we didn't remove them, even afterwards, even
the men with their scruffy beards and brave faces.

I kept some of your ashes to bury beneath the lilac,
then marked your grave with a butterfly made of beads.

This morning its wings are white with hoarfrost
and ice crystals are melting into the earth.

III. Inheritance

Polishing the Spoons

Polishing the silver spoons that belonged to my grandmother, then my mother, and now me, I picture us standing at the kitchen sink absorbed in cleaning, our satisfaction in seeing the black tarnish come off on the rag.

> shining from
> the concave mirror
> distorted reflections

My grandmother wears a long dress with an apron splashed with stains from cooking for eight children. Her auburn hair is braided and coiled on top of her head. Her thick fingers move slowly, thoroughly, over each spoon.

> worrying about
> the summer tobacco crop
> spilt gravy

Mother is wearing a 1950s housedress, faded and tattered from too many presses through the ringer. Her short, black hair forms tendrils in the New England heat. She has taken off her diamond and laid it on the counter. Her once-beautiful hands are dry and puckered. She scrubs quickly.

> thinking about
> the pail of dirty diapers
> and how she'll finally leave him

I'm wearing white shorts and a cobalt blue top from Bali, laced with silver threads. I don't own an apron. Barefooted, blond hair wound on top of my head, I polish the spoons while waiting for the kettle to boil. Rubber gloves protect my lacquered nails.

> reflecting
> that I have no one
> to leave these spoons to

Regrets Only

I'm sorry for the cilantro turning to liquid
in the refrigerator that weeps a puddle
every night while we sleep

for not smoking a last reefer with Aunt Helen
before she died—not kissing her neck
that smelled of geraniums

and, while we're on the topic of flowers,
I also regret making "hamburgers"
with Hazel Tombs' hydrangeas.

I'm sorry that my sweaters
are riddled with holes
because I refuse to use mothballs

sorry for the cardamom seeds that get stuck
in my teeth before I spit them out
on the cracked sidewalk

and for stepping on those cracks
when I was mad at Mother—her back
broken now when I truly love her.

I'm also sorry for the door that creaks
at midnight when I crawl into bed—
you asleep, not sorry for anything

sorry for the branch that breaks
in the old-growth forest
with no one to hear it die

sad for my father, whose last breath
was the taste of bitter antiseptic
in the back of an ambulance.

Most of all, I'm sorry that icicles have to melt,
that mud must harden, and that my heart
in middle age can do neither.

The Good Sister

We're drinking Black Russians and reliving childhood memories:
the day we left Daddy, how we tamed the barn cats at the farm,
the reek of Uncle Ralph's cigars.

Soon she begins her drunken lament:
Everyone always said that you were the smart one
and I was the pretty one. What good did that do me?

Every time we meet, it's the same refrain:
Your life's so wonderful. Mine's horrible. Why do I have
such rotten luck? I try so hard, but nothing works out for me.

At midnight, after popcorn and tears, she begs me to sleep
next to her, like in the old days when I had to check
under the bed for the Bogeyman so she could sleep.

I'm such a good person. Every week I go to the animal shelter
and I hold the kittens and talk to them and say good-bye
to every one of them before they're killed.

And for the rest of the night I lie awake—haunted
by kittens clinging to her pink angora sweater,
the stench of their fur burning into ashes

as my sister, my irreproachable sister,
snores contentedly beside me.

I Always Wanted a Purse That Clicked Open and Shut

like Mother's black linen one with the silver clasp, or Aunt Jean's handbag from Bermuda that smelled of hemp and Juicy Fruit gum, or Aunt Betty's, made from crocodile skin because she'd married a rich man.

I snooped through all those purses to learn what it was like to be a woman. Mother's were full of tiny Avon lipstick samplers in different shades of red. Sometimes they'd come open and stain the lining—like blood, like beets, like other reds I hated. She always carried a small vial of Arpege that she dabbed on her wrists whenever she went out to PTA meetings.

I loved her handkerchief, embroidered with a cardinal, and the pill case with hand-painted bluebells. I clicked it open and shut, never daring to take a pill. Pills would make you crazy, like Aunt Helen who drank her wine in a goblet and flicked her monogrammed lighter when she lit a Lucky Strike. I wanted that lighter. I wanted her purse, too, a shoulder bag with beads and a gold lamé chain.

When the four Cembalisty sisters got together, I'd sit at the table and wait for one of them to open her purse and take out a silver compact to powder her nose or to reapply lipstick. Or for someone to reach into a hidden pocket and snap open the silver-plated locket with a black-and-white photo of their brother Albert who died in the war. Sometimes there would be baby rattles or hard peppermint candies. And, always, clean cotton gloves tucked into the outside pocket.

My handbag is a plain black leather Coach bag bought on sale at the Woodburn Outlets. Inside are: various Revlon lipsticks I apply without a mirror; house, car, and mailbox keys; a wallet full of plastic cards;

a cell phone; and a hairbrush. I have no daughters or nieces to snoop through my purse. And there's no longer that satisfying click when I slide open the metal zipper with its line of well-behaved teeth.

Feral

Think twice about what you bring into your house,
like the muskrat coat stitched from a hundred pelts.

Wearing it into the woods, you turn feral. Eyes
glint like stars heaved into a bog. Your fur body

roils inside the globe of a November night, paws
snatch at blackened fruit fallen to the ground.

This is the coat that wore my aunt. This is the coat
that outlived my aunt, my godmother, who gave me

ribbon candy at Christmas. To please her, I snapped
off a ruffle of cinnamon and clove and held it sharp

beneath my tongue. That night, I crept into the forest,
tore off a strip of birch bark, and licked its chalky dust.

Today I am shrugging off the weight of pelts,
releasing all those dead muskrats.

Look how the fur flies back to the stream.
Watch the wounded muskrat heave up mud

to recreate the earth. Smell its musky pelt.
Wipe clean your blood-red claws.

In the Garden

Once I planted dahlias bulbs upside down. Their roots
strained upward like albino worms, like legs of beetles
upturned by young boys who delight in their small power.

There is no pleasure in ignorance and often no punishment.

Those dahlias turned their roots around to the hard place—
toward darkness, where spring rains fell to their deepest level,
where blight could not reach nor sun blemish.

There's something pagan about dahlias—their gaudy colors,
splayed petals. Not so the rhubarb that pokes its bulbous head
up through mud, oblivious as a mole with its ruddy snout.

My grandmother welcomed these nubs, protected them
with mulch through an uncertain spring. And when the stalks
leafed out, she cut the rhubarb with her dull and rusty knife.

I gathered the stems. They smelled of cold earth and wax.
Later, Nana and I would sit side by side at the kitchen table
and dip them into the sugar bowl.

I should have watched her: the digging, planting, and feeding.

This afternoon, I pulled up ornamental grasses, flattened
and brown, and among them green sprouts—I took those out
too, not knowing what they were until later I remembered:
purple scillas.

Like my grandmother, I welcome the soil beneath my nails
my stained and blistered palms. Today I forgive myself
for the dahlias and scillas, for everything I have made struggle.

Inheritance

In the attic of your dead mother's house, you come across
your scrapbook of butterflies: sooty wings, swallowtails,
summer azures sealed in cellophane, their splayed wings

still holding a faint tint of pattern and color—like batik sarongs
scrubbed against rocks and laid out to dry in the Balinese sun
by generations of barefooted women.

Your fingers remember that satisfying crack of the swallowtail's
thorax as you pressed it flat, and those summer evenings
cupping fireflies into a rancid mayonnaise jar, how you punched

tiny air holes in the lid and watched the lightning flicker all night
on your bedside table. In the morning, they lay heaped
at the bottom, like rubble in a graveyard.

How many things have you killed?

Legions of Japanese beetles plucked from your grandmother's
rose bush, their iridescent copper and green helmets
daring you to disturb their gluttony.

What delight when their squirming legs pricked your fingers
as you plunked them into a can of kerosene. How patriotic
you felt killing those Japs.

And the army of ants, that sharp scent of lemon as you
squashed them with your new white Keds, then wiped
their corpses off in the grass before coming in for supper:

Nana's prize Leghorn that she'd slaughtered, plucked,
and boiled to feed you and your four brothers and sisters.
She never let you see the bloody knife.

Thread Count

These are like the sheets I grew up with, my husband says
as we stretch 100% cotton sheets across our queen-size
mattress. Wrinkles disappear as they settle into place.

I'm obsessed with sheets. I love their silky caress against
bare skin, the pastel ease of good living. When did people
start counting threads: 250-, 500-, and now 1,000-per inch?
How much luxury do you need?

John's mother, with a nursing degree from Yale, ironed
the sheets of her six children. Twelve sheets, six pillowcases.
And another set for the marital bed.

When my mother lay dying in the nursing home on sanitized
sheets, I cleaned out her room at assisted living. Neatly folded
in her bureau drawer, I found six sets of twin-sized sheets.
All threadbare.

And the ones with pastel flowers, faded after forty years—
my sheets from college. So soft and familiar that I wanted
to crawl between them one last time.

Tonight, I don't have the heart to tell my beloved that I bought
these sheets at Value Village. Just like I didn't have the heart
to throw away Mother's—that faint scent of her lavender sachet
as I drove them to Goodwill.

Broken

No matter how broke I was, I always had flowers.
Not long-stemmed roses, but carnations that smelled

like cinnamon, like Thanksgivings spent with my family,
no longer alone in my Boston walk-up worrying

about the old woman across the street staring out
the window with a half bottle of milk on the sill

or Mother sitting at the kitchen table Sunday nights
pasting S&H Green Stamps into books so she could buy

a new Electrolux—cleanliness more important to her
than, well, anything except appearances and privacy.

Even at ninety, when I brought her to Walmart,
she made me wait at the end of the aisle

while she bought Depends. Everything breaks down:
our brittle bones, skin puckered like rotten plums,

split ends in our thinning hair. And heartbreak—
too much heartbreak to bear—one day bleeding

into another and never enough Green Stamps
to replace what's been broken.

Ditching Jesus

Last night I dreamt that I was relaxing in a coffeehouse
when a stranger came over and said: *You look wonderful
sitting there in your fur hat and galoshes with the painting
of Jesus looking down on you.*

How did I manage to sit at that table and not see Jesus
after all those years of parochial school and wanting
to be a nun when I was ten? How did I miss Him when
I'd watched my Bapcha praying to the Twelve Stations
of the Cross on the wall as she ascended her stairs?

Photos of Buddha hang on *my* walls. His bronze statue
sits serenely in full lotus on my altar. Cedar incense fills
the meditation room. I feel comfortable with a religion
that says: *All life is suffering.* There are no surprises.
We play our castanets and die.

Now that I've ditched Jesus, I walk around my house
waiting for a sign that I have chosen the right faith:
the smell of *miso* soup, a crane flying overhead,
someone saying *arigato*—yes, thank you—on the radio.

Things My Aunt Helen Told Me

Keep your feet on the ground, even though you long to fly.
Everyone knows that ugly ducklings belong in the water.

Don't lick the dew off a cabbage leaf. It gives you false hope.
Its destiny is to be boiled in an iron pot and eaten by peasants.

Don't ever ask strangers questions in an elevator.
You may get answers that will let the horses back into the barn.

Happiness may sit next to you on the park bench, but once
you notice it, it will fly away on the wings of pigeons.

Beware of heirlooms. The grape snipper and pickle forks
will sever your connection with the present.

Never believe what a mime tells you. He knows how
to tell lies with his fingertips and in the slope of his pelvis.

Someday soon, you will meet a man in a chenille bathrobe
who will offer you a cigar. Stop searching for the perfect lover.

When you plan your future, be sure to include lace and licorice
and don't forget to replace the light bulbs in your head.

Elbow of Desire

Sometimes the clouds never open.
They just tumble past you
with their mares' tails
and sonic booms
and the trees quake
with expectation
though their limbs
have been hacked
by the woodcutter.

Crows come at dusk
balancing on the needles
of firs. Their ink-black feathers
unfurl, lifting them into darkness.
The sky closes its fist.

We travel a long way down
to the elbow of desire.
Sometimes it raises
our greedy hand to beckon,
to gorge, to smother the loneliness
that travels like fleas across the soft
tendrils of our arms.

Sometimes it jabs into the solar plexus
of remembrance, where flowers bloom
from a belly of tears.
Or rests on a table
bracing a head full of longing,
like seeds rattling in a gourd.

Sometimes desire breaks through
the night sky, vain as Cassiopeia's elbows
gripping the arms of her celestial throne
at the edge of the Milky Way—
hanging upside down
to learn humility.

Both Sides Now

In the yard, everything has turned brown.
Leaves are lying on the compliant earth

just as you did in summer, listening to
the chatter of women and birds.

When you are happy, even the flurry
of a hummingbird's wings is soothing.

Later you hear the murmur of approval
from the fridge as you select carrots,
onions, and broccoli from its cold belly.

You are making soup, singing along with
Joni Mitchell on one of your old records:

I've looked at life from both sides now
and you're twenty-five again, blue-eyed

California-tanned, your voice clear as
the prism casting rainbows on the wall

pure as the breeze in the redwood forest
where you forage for mushrooms and sorrel

and then sit for awhile in the tree house
where you made love on summer afternoons.

You don't yet know how happy you are—
how your body can leap into midair

and land soft as milkweed fluff.
How everything you ask for
comes to you wrapped with a ribbon.

When you look into the mirror,
you do not yet see your Mother's face.

Back then, you knew that whatever you put
into the cooking pot would be delicious—

the scent of forest, alchemy of fire
and spring water nourishing each other.

Even now, forty years later, as you stand
barefoot in your yellow kitchen,

your mouth opens in a small *O*
round and red as rosehips

that remain on the bush
after the rose has fallen.

Honey

I dream that I visit Mother in the last days of her life as she lies
in bed naked, comfortable being naked as she never was when
she was alive, her back tan and supple like Katherine Hepburn's
in *The Philadelphia Story* and I'm naked too as we compare
stomachs—how our fat is below our belly buttons, not above
like a shelf that can fold over things and hold them fast—and
when she looks down to see how much pubic hair I have left,
I cannot bring myself to look at hers and before I know it
she's smiling at my raised skin tag, brown like hers and in
the same place (the fold of our left thighs) discovered one
afternoon sunning together by the pool, never imagining
winter or old age or even this dream years after she's gone
where she's offering me a jar of honey saying
Rub this into your skin. It will keep you forever young.

I Love the Way

you separate skin from peach
    knife blade sharp and clean against flesh
      your tongue sliding over lower lip
        in rapt anticipation

          the way you peel back
           that last clinging strip
             with your slender fingers
              then, fling it aside

                holding the naked globe
                  in your hollowed palm
                    before raising it
                        in communion to your lips

                    then taking that first bite
                  a sacrament to pleasure
              peach juice dripping down your chin
            eyes closing out the world

          you press your hands
        deeper into creamy flesh
     as your mouth devours
the splendor.

Nymph in the River

Johnson, Vermont

Now finally,
after so many days,
I am part of this river
naked sylph, smooth
   white boulder
     stretching fully
       to receive and let go
         the wash of water.

There is danger too—
the slippery rocks I fasten onto
   hoping they will hold in the current
     trusting that they will not
       tumble down river
         to their next resting place.

Oh, the coolness sluicing my hair
   again and again, like seaweed
     splayed in the currents.

Like Aphrodite,
I am reckless with pleasure
   the heat on my lips
     then, face down, I want to go
       deeper into flesh
         wedged between rocks
           far from shore
             intoxicated
               by the smell of water.

Song of Gratitude

Love the Kamo River, its waters turned blue
from rinsing the indigo dyes of kimonos.

Love the hummingbirds.

Love the koi who swim like kings
even though, without their glitter,
they'd be only mouth and tail.

Love the katsura tree with its multiple trunks
and heart-shaped leaves.

Admire the anteater and its endurance,
carrying its armor for a lifetime.

Rejoice in the green of a kingfisher's wing
or the deep purple skin of an eggplant.

Delight in the color of dusk when sun breaks
through the scum of clouds and a rabbit
peers out of his hutch.

Love your mother who always wears
her favorite dress when she comes to you

in dreams and give thanks to the lilac bush
that blooms from her ashes.

Love also the sounds of trucks without mufflers
the breath of drunkards returning home

and the chorus of spring peepers, reminding you
that you are not alone.

Delight in waking from a deep sleep to hear
the snoring of your husband beside you—

alive, yes, still alive.

Vespers

This is how I end my day—
hands clasped around a hose
sinuous as a serpent.

An arc of water forms a halo
from the lingering light, a font
of absolution in my chapel

of roses, lavender, hydrangeas.
It raises up lowly, hidden things
crouched all day beneath the darkness

of leaves—slugs, snails, mosquitoes
and a triumvirate of moths, white
and ethereal as the Holy Ghost.

Tomato plants droop from the burden
of their fruit. Raspberry vines twist
and turn toward the sun, embed

their thorns in my hands. Lavender,
rosemary, and thyme bow down
as they are anointed with water.

This is how I end my day:
with blues and yellows and softening greens
with water tempering the day's dust

with a choir of grosbeaks
singing *Amen! Amen!*
It is so. It is so.

About the Author

Margaret Chula grew up on her grandparent's tobacco farm on the banks of the Connecticut River where she explored eighty acres of woods and meadows. In her thirties, she traveled around the world with her husband, John, and then settled in Kyoto for twelve years, where she taught English and creative writing at universities. Maggie has published seven collections of poetry, including *Grinding my ink*, which received the Haiku Society of America Book Award. She has been a featured speaker and workshop leader at writers' conferences throughout the United States, as well as in Poland, Canada, and Japan. In 2010, she was appointed Poet Laureate for Friends of Chamber Music in Portland, Oregon. She also served as President of the Tanka Society of America from 2011-2015. Grants from Oregon Literary Arts and the Regional Arts & Culture Council have supported collaborations with poets, artists, musicians, photographers, and dancers. She lives in Portland, Oregon, where she hikes, gardens, swims, and creates flower arrangements for every room of the house.